Does GOD Ever Speak through CATS?

David Evans

Third Printing 2021

10 9 8 7 6 5 4 3 2 1

ISBN 0-929422-99-6
Library of Congress Catalog Card Number 2006900130

Published by The Jonah Press, Sherman Oaks, California

Book layout, cover design, and illustrations by Ernie Weckbaugh of Casa Graphics, Inc., Burbank, California.

"Being a PK myself (Preacher's Kid), I found David Evans' story of discovering his Faith through one of God's most beautiful creatures both inspiring and touching."

Jayne Meadows Allen

To Sally

Not only was she a fun and worthy companion through all the events of this book, but she was the one who provided the key ingredients. She introduced me to Mehitabel, and she took me to church that long ago Easter Sunday.

TABLE OF CONTENTS

PART ONE

PART TWO

Thank You!

Nothing occurs in a vacuum, and this book is no exception. Along the way there were many people who helped me directly and indirectly, or gave me encouragement when I needed it. I am deeply in their debt. They each blessed me in their different and unique ways. So I am taking this opportunity to say “Thank You!” to each of the following people:

Jayne Meadows Allen, Kathe Orrison Labby, Ida Baur, Betsy Caprio, Jeri Ferris, Susan Ring Harris, Pat Dorsey, Ralph Evans, Katharine Evans, Ernie Weckbaugh, Patty Weckbaugh, Mike Ames, Marlies Amarca, and Dan Whims.

This isn't everybody, of course. Any list of this kind can never be truly complete. But the people I have listed here have been extremely helpful, giving, and encouraging. Thanks so much! I couldn't have done it without you.

David Evans

Introduction

Eleven years ago, my wife Sally and I moved into a little Spanish house on Dorothy Street on the West Side of Los Angeles. It was an economy move really. Up until that time I had worked as a free lance writer in television (for *the Monkees* and *Love American Style,* among other things). But TV had become increasingly frustrating to me, and I wanted to move into some other kind of writing. The trouble was, I hadn't figured out yet exactly what it would be. So my income at that point was very uncertain.

The house on Dorothy Street was ideal. The rent was low and the house was tremendously charming. It was a very small two-bedroom house in the classic Spanish style. It had high ceilings, a tile roof, a blue stone floor, an enclosed patio in the back, and a fireplace.

The reason the rent was low was because nothing worked in the house. It had been built over sixty years before and was in considerable disrepair. The wiring was antiquated, the plumbing didn't work well, there were leaks in the roof, and the wood on the windows was so deteriorated that they wouldn't close properly. But it was a wonderful house, truly beautiful if you didn't mind inconvenience.

It was an incredibly rich eleven years in many ways. Thousands of things happened. But there were two primary threads that wove through the entire time.

One thread was my exploration of Christianity.

I grew up as the son of a Presbyterian minister, a PK, "Preacher's Kid." Like many preacher's kids I went as far in the opposite direction from religion as I could. I stayed away from church for years. Then one Easter Sunday, just two months before Sally and I moved to Dorothy Street, I went to church and had a powerful conversion experience.

The content of the experience was very vague really. I didn't know exactly what to do, and I was filled with more questions than answers. All I knew was that, some way or other God had claimed me to be his, and that my life would never be the same again.

So, one of the primary themes of my life during the eleven years on Dorothy Street was my exploration and growth in the Christian faith.

Another primary theme during my time in the Dorothy Street house was my relationship with a cat that was living in the back yard when we moved in.

Amazingly enough, as time went on I began to see that these two things, my faith and the cat, had a lot to do with each other. In fact, one day I realized that the cat was actually a parable. This is the book I wrote to tell that story: *Does GOD ever speak through CATS?*

David Evans
Los Angeles

bridge-building.com

Part One

1

Autobiography of a Cat Hater

When Sally and I moved into the house on Dorothy Street I despised cats. I'm not sure why exactly, but I did. I hated them. Whenever a cat approached me I would pull away. Cats seemed unfriendly and unpleasant. I didn't want to have anything to do with them.

Consequently I wasn't too pleased when I discovered that there was a stray cat living in the overgrown back yard of the house we had moved into. When we were bringing our furniture in I saw the cat on the sill of the back window, looking into the kitchen. I made a face, yelled, flapped my arms, and the cat jumped off and disappeared into the back yard somewhere.

There was a lot of room for it to disappear into. The back yard was big. There was a garage, a small rickety out-building in the back, an untended garden area filled with weeds, a long wild hedge, several overgrown bushes and fruit trees, and all kinds of secret cul de sacs and hiding places. Of *course* there was a cat living in the back yard. It was the perfect place for one.

Luckily, because there were so many hiding places in the back I hardly ever saw the cat. Once it found out I didn't like it, it kept its distance. Days and weeks would go by without my ever seeing it.

Once in a while we would see it walking slowly and purposefully through the front yard near the house. "Patrolling," Sally called it. The cat was gray with tiger stripes that formed a circle on its side. I didn't have a campaign of active belligerency against the cat. I didn't need to. I hardly ever saw it. So my original feelings of active hostility toward the cat began to subside.

In fact, my feelings of hostility toward the cat had eased up so much, that one time when Sally suggested putting out some chicken scraps for the cat, I said it was okay. As long as she put the plate way at the back of the yard by the ramshackled little house. As long as it was far enough away, I didn't care what happened. The cat and I had a truce.

It turned out that the reason the cat kept its distance so well was because it was afraid of people. Sally would take a piece of chicken out to the cat with the idea of petting it when it came up for the food. (The oldest trick in the book.) But the cat wouldn't come up. Not while Sally was there. It would watch from way off to the side and then it would run up after Sally was gone.

Sometimes the cat would stay up on the roof of the little house until Sally was a safe distance away. Then it would slowly come down the fig tree to the ground and run over to the food.

So the cat became a challenge. Sally began a campaign to pet the cat, and I got caught up in it. Not because of the cat, but because of the challenge.

And it *was* a challenge. The cat always kept its distance, wary and afraid. Time after time Sally and I would crouch down near the fig tree by the little house with a plate of scraps, trying to bring the cat near enough to pet. And time after time the cat resisted. It stayed up on the roof of the little house and waited until we were gone.

An interesting thing happened to me during this time. I had such a strong desire to succeed in Sally's and my enterprise of petting the cat that the desire affected my other thinking. Without my quite realizing it, I began to really *want* to pet the cat. Even apart from the challenge.

One day it began to look possible. Instead of staying on the roof of the little house while we crouched with the food, the cat climbed a little way down the fig tree. It wasn't far, but the cat had definitely made a move toward us! Sally and I were really excited. The plan was working. We knew now that it was just a matter of time before we could pet the cat.

Every day from then on, when we brought the cat's food out, it came a little farther down the fig tree. One day it reached the ground while we were still holding the dish. From that point on, every day the cat came a little closer and a little closer.

Then finally one day it happened. We petted it.

It didn't last long. The cat darted away almost immediately. But we *did* pet it. It was an incredible experience. A culminating victory after a great deal of time, effort, and patience.

I didn't realize it at the time, but from that moment on I was hopelessly lost.

Sally and I and the cat moved into a new relationship that lasted for the next two or three months. My hostility was gone but I still had a lot of resistance. It was all too new and strange. The cat was skittery, but the truth was, I was skittery too.

The cat was now free to go anywhere in the back yard or on the patio, but it had its limits. I wouldn't allow it in the house. It was strictly an outdoor cat. We petted it every day now and it became steadily tamer. Then one day I had one of the most wonderful experiences anyone can have in this world. Right in the middle of petting the cat, it started purring!

I named the cat Mehitabel and that made it official. She was our cat.

I was still reluctant to let Mehitabel in the house. I agreed with Sally that she could come into the kitchen, but no further.

Not long after that I served on a committee to judge some television programs and make selections for an award. There was a huge amount of footage to watch. I was gone almost the entire weekend from extremely early until extremely late. When the whole thing was finally over and I got back home and took a look around, I found Mehitabel curled up on the couch in the living room.

I took immediate action. I petted her.

She's had complete run of the house ever since.

I named the cat Mehitabel after a character in a favorite book of mine, "Archie and Mehitabel," by Don Marquis. It's the story of a cat named Mehitabel who tells her fabulous life story to a cockroach named Archie, who types it all up.

Because Archie is so little (he's only the size of a bug, after all) the only way he can type is to climb all the way up to the carriage of the typewriter and throw himself down on whatever letter he wants to type. Needless to say, it takes him a long time to type anything.

Archie in the book is involved in typing up the story of Mehitabel, and it's quite a story. Mehitabel, the cat, claims to be the reincarnation of an Egyptian princess. Mehitabel regales Archie with stories of her love affairs and her fabulous adventures in the pharaoh's court in Ancient Egypt. Mehitabel is a sort of feline Scheherazade.

There was a cockeyed logic to my choosing the name. In the book, the Egyptian Mehitabel had a writer as a companion. And, since I have been a free lance writer most of my life, the Mehitabel on Dorothy street had a writer as a companion too. So there was a rightness to the name.

Actually, it was because of the fact that I am a writer that Mehitabel and I got to be such great buddies. I was at home a great deal, working on writing assignments. Mehitabel was home. So our lives became happily intertwined.

I would work at the typewriter. If I wanted to mull over an idea or a phrase, I would often get up and wander out to the back yard where Mehitabel was. Then I'd kneel down and give her chin a scratch.

Other times I would be working at the typewriter, and Mehitabel would be curled up on the typewriter stand. Or on my desk right beside it. Or on my lap, purring. Mehitabel and I were inseparable. We were together day and night. In fact, many nights she slept on the bed and I went to sleep to the sound of her purring. I loved her and we were great buddies. She was the focus of a great deal of my time and attention.

But there was also another focus.

I was in the midst of one of the biggest changes of my life. For the previous twenty years, from my teens until the time I moved to Dorothy Street, I had had a great deal of hostility to Christianity and churches. (This is a very common problem among people whose father's are ministers.) I hated everything having to do with Christianity.

But about a month before we moved to Dorothy Street, on Easter, I went to church with Sally at her urging. I didn't want to, and I didn't believe in it at that point, but I reluctantly agreed to go.

What happened to me was amazing. It's hard to describe it really, but what I experienced was a religious conversion. As I was sitting in the pew some words came into my mind and my whole being. I didn't actually "hear" the words with my ears; I *experienced* them. The words were these: "You belong here. Work it out."

The words seemed strange and enigmatic, but I knew without question that they were from God. And when I walked out of church that Easter I knew that God had claimed me, and from then on, in some fundamental way, my life was completely changed.

I didn't know how exactly. And I wasn't really what I would call a "believer" then. At that point I didn't know what I believed. All I knew was that I was changed. I'd been claimed. From now on everything was different.

I was filled with questions. They weren't questions of doubt. They were questions of curiosity. All of a sudden my existence had veered off down a different cosmic path. I was headed toward a new life. I wanted to find out all about it.

What is God? Who is Jesus? What does it mean to be the "Son of God"? Is there a Heaven? Is the Bible really true? What does it mean to be a "Christian"? How does it all relate to me personally? What am I supposed to do *now*?

I began reading the Bible a great deal, hungry, looking for answers.

The Bible seemed fascinating and wonderful, but strange. It talked about strange things like forgiving your enemies! The Bible said paradoxically that the only way you could *gain* your life was to *lose* it! It all sounded so incomprehensible and impossible. I thought about it often. Christianity was the focus of a great deal of my energy and attention.

So, after I moved onto Dorothy Street there were two things that were often in my thoughts: a cat named Mehitabel and the Christian faith.

Then one day I realized that my whole relationship with Mehitabel was like a kind of parable. I had an enemy: cats. But (by a fluke, really), instead of continuing to *hate* that enemy I reached out in *love* toward it, and I received tremendous joy and blessings as a result. Blessings I couldn't even have imagined were possible!

The whole experience with Mehitabel had a profound effect on my religious life and thinking.

Right at the time when I was reading passages in the Bible telling us to love our enemies, I was experiencing a parable in my own life that proved the truth and goodness of that commandment to me.

Now admittedly, cats are not people. (Remember, you read it here first.) The Bible does not tell us to love *cats*. It tells us to love *people*. And in a sense, love toward a cat may seem to be a trivial case. But the impact of the experience and its implications went far beyond my relationship with my cat. Trivial though the experience may have been, it was nonetheless a powerful illustration of the fact that, if we can substitute love for hate in our relationships with our enemies, wonderful things can happen.

And, if I could take that same kind of risk I took with a cat and forgive my *human* enemies, who knows what wonderful blessings might result? The experience with Mehitabel changed my viewpoint toward my human relationships. It helped me to see those relationships with a greater sense of their possibility. And the experience gave me a much deeper appreciation for the Bible. I had seen a small but dramatic proof of the power of one of the Bible's great teachings.

The disciples had signs and proofs of Christ's power. So did all the people who saw him preach and teach. They witnessed healings, miraculous wine, impossible loaves and fishes, and an amazing walk on the water.

We have proof of Christ's power too. Proof in our lives. Signs all around us. We all have personal parables in each one of our lives. Parables of God's truth and love.

Sometimes those proofs and parables come into our lives in the strangest and most mysterious ways. For example, who would ever imagine that a person could have a religious experience because of a gray tabby cat?

2

God Holds the Patent on Cats

In ten years time with Mehitabel, she never ceased to delight me. I loved to look at her. She always seemed to me to be a marvel of visual design. Her whiskers, her paws, her fur, her tail, her funny pointed ears! Think of the astonishing invention that was involved in Creation. God not only *made* cats, he *invented* them. He created the whole *idea* of cats!

If I look out in the back yard, all I see is a back yard, a rather unkempt one at that. But Mehitabel would go out into the back yard and suddenly it became a wonderland. There was a multitude of strange scents to investigate, clumps of weeds to explore, and grasshoppers and lizards to stalk.

Mehitabel had a million special places in the back. Places to hide, places to sleep, places to hunt, places to perch, places to sun herself, places to climb, places to roll in the dirt, places to wash in, places to watch from, and places to explore.

She loved to lie down in the back. If it was a cool day, she would warm herself in the sun. If it was sunny and hot, she would luxuriate in the shade. She could fine-tune the heat and cold better than a Nobel Prize winner in thermodynamics.

I always loved to watch Mehitabel jump.

The house on Dorothy Street is a little Spanish house. It has rooms in the front and on both sides, and a patio in the middle of the back. There is a five-foot wall at the end of the patio, and a gate that opens to the back yard. The thick adobe wall at the end of the patio was always Mehitabel's favorite jumping place. She would crouch at the bottom and then leap up in an effortless blur. She was beautiful and amazing to watch.

Often, from the wall she would take another leap onto the roof and then walk across the tiles. She would then either sit beside the chimney at the peak of the roof, or she would continue *over* the front roof and then jump down into the front yard.

I always loved watching Mehitabel walk across the roof. She looked very grand and majestic. One reason was because it was a tile roof. The tiles were curved, so that she would always walk forward a step, and then have to walk a catch-up step. Walk forward a step, then walk another catch-up step. The effect was very stately.

I particularly liked watching her walk on the roof at night. I remember one night I was sitting on the patio in the dark, enjoying the air and listening to a Mozart piano concerto that was coming from the living room. Mehitabel jumped up on the wall, then up onto the roof, and then began making her way slowly toward the front.

It was a summer night and the sky was clear and filled with stars. When Mehitabel walked along the roof I could see stars all around her. There were even stars underneath her, between her front legs and her back legs. She was like a furry constellation in the sky.

Mehitabel had as many special places *inside* the house as she did outside. She loved to be *up* on things, *on top* of things, or *inside* things. She was endlessly inventive when it came to finding surprising new places to sleep.

My arrangement with Sally has always been that, whenever we send packages off, she wraps them, and then I take them to the U.P.S. So, after she gets the packages wrapped, she puts them in the middle of the living room floor to remind me to mail them.

Mehitabel would *always* lie on top of the packages. It didn't matter how big they were or how small. She loved to lie on them.

And she loved to get inside things. I always had to keep the drawers closed in my file cabinet. Otherwise she'd get inside. And sometimes she would get inside and chew on my old *Monkees* scripts. (Everybody's a critic.)

Once, when I left the towel drawer open in the bathroom, she spent the entire night in with the towels, purring.

Many times Mehitabel would get up on Sally's or my lap. I have the memory of many happy evenings in the fall and winter, sitting in front of a fire in the fireplace, talking to Sally with Mehitabel curled up on Sally's lap.

Or curled up on my lap, when I was sitting up late at night in my reclining chair reading.

One of the best experiences of all was when Mehitabel would sometimes hop up on the bed with Sally and me and go to sleep with us. It is a wonderful luxury to drift off to sleep between soft sheets to the sound of a purring cat.

One of the peculiarities of my sleep is the fact that I always get up at least once in the middle of the night, every night, and I have all my life. The reason for this is the fact that I have three kidneys. I know this may sound odd, but it is nonetheless true. It doesn't cause me any real problems. The only way it affects me is that it tends to cause my system to generate extra fluid. Consequently, I always have to empty my bladder in the middle of the night.

It never really bothers me or interferes with my sleep. I awaken just enough to get up, go into the bathroom, and then come back to bed. Then I drift off back to sleep again. If full consciousness is like a brightly-lit room, then my middle-of-the-night consciousness is kind of like having a night light on. It's very low-powered and dim.

Some time very early in the game Mehitabel learned my schedule and began using it to her advantage. If she wanted to go outside in the middle of the night, she would wait until my sleep started getting restless and I was about to wake up. Then she would jump up on the table across from my side of the bed and start to meow. I would drowsily get up out of bed, pick Mehitabel up, take her to the door and let her out, go to the bathroom, and then go back to bed.

And once Mehitabel established that pattern, she expanded on it. Before long she meowed every night, *even if she didn't want to go out,* just so she could be picked up and petted. And believe it or not, however strange and foolish it may seem, that's exactly what I did every night. Mehitabel meowed, I got up, and picked her up and petted her. Then I went to the bathroom and went back to bed. "Hugs in the night" was what Sally and I used to call it.

It all happened so gradually and so easily, and at such a dimly conscious time of day, that by the time I realized what was happening, it was far too late to change it. And the truth is, I didn't really want to change it. Because it's a wonderful feeling to get up in the middle of the night and hug a soft purring cat.

One of the words I kept running across in my Bible reading was the word "love." The Bible speaks of God's love for us, our need to love God, and the importance of our loving each other.

But sometimes love is difficult.

It is always hard to love somebody you are having an argument or a dispute with. The human reaction is anger and it is usually very focused, focused on that other person.

But, in a completely different way, it is sometimes hard to love God, too.

One reason, I think, is because God is so enormous, so vastly beyond our comprehension, so abstract.

And sometimes it is hard for us to love God because, although He gives us great blessings, we may experience great frustrations along with those blessings. I know that for myself the time on Dorothy Street has been oddly mixed in that way. I have never felt more personally, maritally, or creatively blessed. But at the same time, I have never been more professionally frustrated.

Life is so complex, and we are buffeted about by so many demands with so many different emotions, that it is often difficult to live with a heart full of thankfulness.

And yet the commandment to love God is the strongest commandment in the Bible. It is the first commandment.

It is the constant theme of the Prophets.

And in the New Testament, in the Gospels of Matthew, Mark, and Luke, the Pharisees asked Jesus what the greatest commandment was. He replied, saying, "You must love the Lord your God with all your heart, with all your soul, and with all your mind."

The question is how do you do it?

I thought about it a great deal.

Then one time in the middle of the night, when Mehitabel got me up, I was standing in the dark, holding her. She felt soft and she was purring. I thought to myself, "What a wondrous creature Mehitabel is. What a marvelous gift. Imagined, created, and given by the Lord. Thank you God, for the gift of a purring cat! Praise God from whom all blessings flow!"

I think my experience with Mehitabel really did help me deepen and enlarge my sense of thankfulness. For one thing, I had a strong sense of her being a *gift.* I often thought of her as "The Gift Cat." A gift given by a *Giver.*

And for another thing, she was such a total delight to me that she seemed a complete and unqualified blessing.

I think it is a very great help in a person's praise/prayer life, to begin by focusing on something simple that one loves completely and without reservation. Even something as small and humble as a tabby cat.

...And *then,* to constantly strive to enlarge on that sense of thankfulness, and to ever deepen one's love of the Lord.

I know Mehitabel was a help to me in that way. Because holding a soft, purring cat in the darkness helped me realize that God loves us and gives us all "Hugs in the Night."

3

Love and Fear

We never knew exactly what Mehitabel's life was like before we met her on Dorothy Street. But there were clues.

One clue was the fact that she had a long surgical scar on her abdomen. We knew she had belonged to someone else earlier in her life, and she was involved enough in their life that they took her to the vet at least once.

Another clue to Mehitabel's past was the fact that, whenever Sally and I got out the suitcases to take a trip, she always got very upset.

Our guess was that the people Mehitabel was living with moved away, and Mehitabel got left behind in the process. However it happened, the experience of abandonment had a very traumatic effect on her. It made her very fearful whenever we got ready to take a trip.

Luckily, it just so happens that Sally and I have done very little travelling in the last ten years. And those few trips were generally very short. Whenever we did go anywhere, we always made arrangements to have someone around to give Mehitabel fresh food and water while we were gone. I tried to reassure her every way I could that we would be back, but it was still difficult. Her fear of being abandoned ran very deep.

Still another clue to Mehitabel's past was the fact that she always ran from strangers. If she was in the house and someone came to the door, she would bolt for the back door and the safety of the back yard. She was afraid of people.

Sally and I always assumed that the reason for her fear was the fact that she had been mistreated somewhere along the way. Whatever the experience was, her fear was deep-seated. Long after she had become incredibly tame with Sally and me, and was getting "hugs in the night," she would still dart for the back whenever anyone else came in.

One of the hardest times for her was at Christmas.

For Sally and me on Dorothy Street, Christmas was always one of the best times of the year. There were parties, fun visits, wonderful church services, Handel's *Messiah*, good friends, evenings by the fireside, Dickens' *Christmas Carol,* and the heightened sense of blessedness that comes from the advent and nativity of our Lord.

One of the highpoints of each Christmas for Sally and me has always been the annual visit of Sally's mother, Momma Ethel. Momma Ethel always comes to visit for about two weeks every Christmas. She is very fun to be around. She has a great sense of humor and a wonderful spirit of enthusiasm. She greatly adds to the enjoyment of each Christmas Season.

But every year, from the moment Momma Ethel arrived from the airport, till the moment two weeks later when she left, Mehitabel would always exile herself to the back yard. It happened the same way, year after year.

One Christmas about four years ago, Momma Ethel left the Colorado snow drifts, and arrived in California to find the weather in the balmy eighties. What better way to enjoy it than by having lunch in the back yard?

For several days Sally and her mother ate together in the back. A couple of times they sat down only a few feet away from Mehitabel, and Mehitabel didn't seem to mind.

One day, when Mehitabel was lying close by, Sally's mother put her plate down on the ground. To their amazement, Mehitabel sauntered over and started to lick the plate. Then Momma Ethel petted her, as though they had always been the best of friends.

And that night, when Sally and I walked Momma Ethel to her room and turned on the light, there was Mehitabel, curled up on the bed, purring! Mehitabel had gotten over her fear. She and Momma Ethel were friends.

Of course, Mehitabel hadn't gotten over *all* her fears. It just meant that she had become friends with Momma Ethel. But she was definitely on the way. She still ran away from other people after that, but she made more and more friends. Almost always with people who came to the house often. Several people petted her. It took a long time, but her fear gradually receded more and more into the past.

The same was true with her fear of being left behind. That also took a long time. We had to come back to her enough times for her to realize that we *would* come back. Gradually that fear too began to recede.

I often think about the night Mehitabel first got up on Momma Ethel's bed. Sally and I and Momma Ethel have talked about it many times since then. It impressed us all and stayed in our minds because it was such an amazing experience. Here was Mehitabel, who for years had run from Momma Ethel in fear, now curled up on her bed purring! It was a real breakthrough.

It is exciting to see a breakthrough or to be present at one. It is a real celebration. Seeing Mehitabel on Momma Ethel's bed next to her was amazing. It gave us all the feeling that, if *this* can happen, *anything* is possible.

But of course there was a reason for it, and the reason was love.

One thing Sally and I always gave Mehitabel was a lot of love. It was easy to do because we did love her. But Mehitabel knew it. She lived in an environment of love, and it was in that environment that her breakthrough occurred. I believe many breakthroughs are accomplished through love. Maybe all of them are.

There are many breakthroughs recorded in the Bible. They occur in a variety of ways, through the agencies of dreams, angels, rainbows, whirlwinds, apocalyptic visions, healings, and the blinding light that felled Saul on the road to Damascus.

And God's abiding love was at the heart of each of them.

There are breakthroughs in all of our lives. Breakthroughs of the mind. Breakthroughs of the heart. Breakthroughs of the spirit. I believe that it is God who is moving through all of them, calling us, helping us, healing us, rescuing us.

I had a wonderful breakthrough dream about three or four years ago. It concerned a man I knew several years before, whom I haven't seen since.

He was a neighbor of mine and lived in the same apartment building. He had been in an automobile accident three years before and was left a paraplegic, unable to walk. He spent all his time in a wheel chair.

I had never been around a paraplegic before and I found it very distressing. I developed a tremendous fear of paralysis. The thought of it filled me with anxiety and dread, and the fear continued for years.

Then one night I had a dream.

It was a very brief dream, but it was extremely vivid. My paralyzed neighbor was in the dream. He was sitting in his wheel chair. Then, slowly, very dramatically, *he stood up and walked away from the wheel chair!*

I don't remember anything else after that, but that was enough. I woke up the next day feeling wonderful, and I haven't been afraid of paralysis since. It's not that I don't have any negative feelings at all about it. I do, of course. Paralysis would be an extremely difficult thing for anyone to cope with. It's just that I'm not terrified of it any more. My fear is gone.

It was a breakthrough. A deliverance.

And there was that long-ago Easter Sunday breakthrough that changed my life forever. God moves through all of our lives with a wondrous and transforming love. Who knows what astonishing and holy breakthroughs lie yet ahead?

4

Three Wishes

There are a great many "new age" religions, human potential therapies, and self-help books these days that all share a common theme. They all teach people, through a wide variety of different techniques, how to get whatever it is they want or desire out of life.

But there is a catch.

The catch is that you may not *know* what it is you truly want or desire.

I know everybody *thinks* they know what it is they want and what it is that will make them happy. I know I always did. That is a very basic human assumption.

But my experience with Mehitabel dramatically proved that just the opposite is true. There is no way in the world I would ever have desired or wished for a cat. In fact I wanted cats to stay away. I *hated* cats!

Yet, when I finally did get a cat, despite all my wishes to the contrary, it turned out to be a wonderfully happy and delightful blessing. Every time I think about that it amazes me.

And what amazes me is not so much that Mehitabel was wonderful, but that she was wonderful *and I never would have guessed or imagined it.*

The implications of this are overwhelming.

Granted, this is the trivial case. We are only talking about a cat here, marvelous though that cat may be. But we are also talking about questions of human will, human knowledge, and human desire. And these are fundamental topics *that affect every aspect of our being.*

The experience with Mehitabel proves to me that at some fundamental level of my life, I don't really know what it is I want, or what it is that will make me happy.

...Even though I always think I do.

Interestingly enough, the classic fairy tales involving "The Three Wishes" make a similar point. In each of these stories a character is magically granted three wishes. He knows exactly what he wants. He then uses up the three wishes, only to discover that he didn't really want what he thought he wanted.

The question that thus emerges is immense: If I don't know what it is I really want, and if I don't know what will make me happy, how can I possibly know how to live my life?

In the midst of all these thoughts and questions, I continued to read the Bible. In fact the questions helped to focus my reading.

At a time when I was aware of my own very flawed and partial human knowledge, I kept reading in the Bible about God's complete and perfect Divine Knowledge. The theme of God's complete knowledge occurs over and over again throughout the Bible, hundreds of times, from Genesis to Revelation.

The book of Psalms constitutes a cycle of hymns praising God and his perfect knowledge. Psalm 139 tells me that God has searched me and known me, and formed all my inward parts while I was being knit together in my mother's womb. The psalm says that even before I existed,

God's eyes saw me. And that before I was formed, all my days were written down in His Book.

In the New Testament Jesus tells us that his Heavenly Father knows everything. He has recorded the distant fall of a sparrow and has even counted the hairs on each of our heads. *I* may not know enough to know what will ultimately make me happy, but *God* does, because he knows everything about me.

The big question then becomes: is there any way we can gain access to that knowledge in order to know how to live a happy life? Amazingly enough the answer the Bible gives to this question is, yes! We *can* use God's perfect knowledge to guide us to a happy life.

But there's a catch.

The catch is that the Bible tells us God's perfect knowledge can only operate in our lives if we turn our lives over to him. I have to follow *God's* will in my life, not my own. Only then can God enter my life and guide me to that happy existence that only he knows how to attain.

Now quite honestly this is a very unsettling idea. My human nature balks at the idea of giving up my will to someone or something outside myself. *I* want to be in charge of my life!

But the idea of turning our lives and wills over to God is one of the primary themes of the Bible. It occurs again and again throughout the scriptures.

In the Book of Genesis, God tells Abraham to leave his homeland and go forth. Abraham goes. He doesn't know where he's going, but he goes anyway. He turns his life over to God and lets God direct his steps.

In the Book of Exodus we read about the life of Moses. One day when Moses was tending his father-in-law's sheep in the land of Midian, God spoke to him from a burning bush. God told Moses to return to Egypt to save his people. Moses was extremely reluctant to go, but he went. He followed God's will rather than his own.

All the other prophets, heroes, and heroines of the Old Testament rose to the state of spiritual heroism by following *God's* will instead of their own.

In the New Testament, when Jesus' disciples asked him how to pray, he taught them the Lord's Prayer: "Our Father, who art in Heaven, hallowed by thy name. Thy kingdom come, thy will be done…"

Thy will be done.

And in the Garden of Gethsemane, as Jesus neared his final hours, Luke tells us that Jesus prayed to his Heavenly Father, saying, "Father, if you will, take this cup from me. Not *my* will, however, but *your* will be done."

So…

Our human knowledge is flawed.

God's knowledge is perfect.

Is there any way we can have access to that perfect knowledge to guide our lives?

Yes.

By turning our lives over to God and letting him guide us.

I came to the realization of all this very slowly. It happened gradually over a period of several years, after I started going to church regularly.

And the marvelous, crazy thing about it all was that Mehitabel played a part in it. Not the key part, or the decisive part. But nonetheless, at a very critical point along the way, she was there as a wonderful, furry, totally unlikely, and miraculous illustration of a very large truth: That there was a great happiness possible for me that was beyond my knowing or imagining.

I'm not sure at what point that I realized the necessity of turning my life over to God, and I'm not sure at what point I began haltingly trying to put it into practice. It was a little like crossing a border while driving at night. I started out in one state, later I found myself in another state, but I'm not sure at what moment the crossover occurred.

But they are different states. It is the difference between being "Christian***ized***" and being a Christian. There is a definite line of demarcation.

Jesus makes this very point in the story of Nicodemus in chapter three of the Book of John. It is a mysterious scene that takes place in the dark of the night. A prominent man named Nicodemus seeks Jesus out to ask him about God and the Kingdom of Heaven. Jesus says to him, "No one can see the Kingdom of Heaven unless he is born again."

The state of belief, the state of salvation, is so radically different from a person's earlier non-believing state, that it is like being born into a completely new existence.

Jesus says that when we are born again we are born in the Spirit. In that new-birthed state of being it is God's Holy Spirit that moves us and guides us.

But before we can be reborn, we must turn our lives over to the Lord. We must believe in Jesus and accept him as our Lord and Savior. Only then can his Holy Spirit come into our lives to guide and transform us.

The truth is, my honest initial reaction to this realization was one of fear. If I turn over my life to God, then that means I am no longer in control of it. That is a very unsettling feeling.

And there is the fear of the unknown. If I truly give my life over to God, then that means I have *no idea* what will happen to me. That really *is* a frightening thought. It makes me feel very vulnerable.

In the midst of this turmoil of thoughts I kept wondering about Abraham.

How did Abraham do it? Didn't he have normal human anxieties? Wasn't he afraid of the unknown? How could he just "go forth" without having any vague idea where God was leading him?

Then I realized the answer.

Faith.

Abraham was able to go forth without fear and with a joyful heart because he had faith. Faith in God, faith in God's goodness, faith that though he, Abraham, walked in ignorance toward an unknown destination, God had a wondrous plan for his life, and would guide all his footsteps.

I suddenly saw the whole concept of faith in a new light. Always before, faith had seemed very abstract to me. I never quite saw how it functioned. But now I could see that it is a crucial and necessary condition for the living of a Christian life.

The only way I can turn my life over to the Lord is to have faith.

Faith in God's redeeming love.

Faith in Jesus' power to completely transform our lives through the Holy Spirit.

But faith in something else too. Faith in "Wonderful Surprises."

The playwrite Ugo Betti once said, "To believe in God is to know that all the rules will be fair, and that there will be wonderful surprises."

Eleven years ago I moved into a new life, in a new house on Dorothy Street. Little did I know what a wonderful furry surprise God had waiting for me in the back yard.

5

Does God Have a Sense of Humor?

I love to think about all the funny things that happened with Mehitabel. She was the source of a multitude of jokes and funny made-up words. And there were several episodes that I always laugh at whenever I think of them.

One episode took place because of some glass beads that Sally bought for the bedroom.

The beads were made of blue glass and were on strings, about six feet long. The strings of beads were designed to hang from a curtain rod above the window. We had about ten strings of them, for each of the two windows in the bedroom. There were different shapes of beads in a repeating pattern on each string. One shape that occurred about every six inches was a big round coat-button-shaped bead (about an inch in diameter).

The beads were very cheap, but I always liked them a lot. They had a nice look, especially early in the morning, when the sun hit them. They were a lovely shade of blue.

Not many days after we put the beads up, Mehitabel started biting them. It was a very funny sight and sound. She would jump up on the table next to the window and start biting one of the big coat-button beads. She wasn't trying to break them or eat them, I don't think. She just seemed to enjoy biting around on them.

As a matter of fact, that was originally the way Mehitabel would wake me up for "hugs in the night." As soon as my sleep started getting restless, she would jump up on the table and start biting the beads, and the crazy "clicking" sound would wake me up.

This went on for months. She must have bitten the beads hundreds of times.

Then one weekend, in the middle of the day, Sally and Mehitabel and I all happened to be in the bedroom at the same time. I was in kind of a comical mood, and I leaned down and *I* bit one of the big coat-button beads.

Mehitabel watched me very intently. I can't imagine what was in her mind, or what it meant to her, but it made a powerful impression on her. Because from that moment on *she never bit the beads again!*

Sally and I have laughed about that ever since. What did it mean to Mehitabel to bite the beads? And why wouldn't she ever do it again once she saw me do it? It was as if she saw me bite the beads, and then thought, "Gee whiz, if even *Dave* does it, how neat can it be?"

One of Mehitabel's greatest passions was fresh liver. The way Sally always fixed liver for her was to cut it up into small pieces with some big scissors that we have, and then pour a little hot water over to it take off the chill.

The scissors had a loud SNICK, SNICK, SNICK sound that Mehitabel quickly associated with liver. It soon got to the place that *whenever* we snicked the scissors, she would come running up and start mooching around, making the funny gargling sound she made whenever she got liver.

Consequently Sally and I went to great pains *not* to snick the scissors if we were using them for other things than cutting liver. *Not* snicking the scissors became an ingrained habit.

In the midst of all this I took a writing job for a while in Orange County about fifty miles away. It was a long commute. It took me an hour to get there in the morning and an hour to come home at night.

One day I was sitting at my desk at work physically cutting and pasting a script together and I had to laugh at myself. Because the habit from home had carried over. I was sitting at my desk, fifty miles away, being very careful not to snick the scissors and alert Mehitabel.

As if she would suddenly run up to my desk in the next county and start mooching for liver!

Last Christmas Sally and I were preparing some packages to send away, so I put a card table up in the living room to give us extra space to work on. The table was up for several weeks.

Somewhere along the way, I tossed a sweater on the table, and Mehitabel immediately started using it as a bed. She was on it constantly for the next week.

Then I wanted to wear the sweater again. So I decided to take the sweater, but replace it with something else as a bed for Mehitabel.

(Yes, of course. Mehitabel was hopelessly spoiled, and I loved every minute of it.)

So I went to the old-clothes-and-rags drawer and rummaged around to see what I could find. I dredged up the perfect solution. It was an old flannel pajama top. It was too torn to wear, but it was very soft and was ideal for Mehitabel.

I put it down on the card table and Mehitabel lay down on it immediately.

When Sally saw Mehitabel lying down on my old flannel top, she just shrugged her shoulders and said, matter-of-factly, "But of course. THE CAT'S PAJAMAS."

That instantly became one of my all-time favorite jokes.

Humor has always been an extremely important part of my life. In fact I have spent most of my adult life as a comedy writer, writing for such TV shows as *the Monkees, Love American Style,* and *the Bill Cosby Show,* among others. So humor is very important to me.

Consequently, when I became a Christian one of my big questions was "What about humor?" Is there any place for humor and laughter in the Christian life? Does God have a sense of humor?

I read the Bible with the question of laughter in mind.

The Bible is, of course, a fundamentally serious book. In fact it is *the* fundamentally serious and holy book. But I believe that there is none-the-less an aspect of humor to it.

For example, consider Chapter 17, Verse 22 in the Book of Proverbs. This is the proverb that says, "A merry heart doeth good like a medicine."

A merry heart!

Or consider the Book of Jonah. Jonah is actually a very funny book. The source of much of the humor in the story is Jonah's incredible folly at thinking he was smarter than God, and could escape him! Jonah is so foolishly human, and so humanly foolish, that he is laughable.

Does God have a sense of humor? The book of John tells us that Jesus and God are one, that Jesus *is* God. So, to find out about God, we look at the life of Jesus. I believe I see some of evidence of a sense of humor in Jesus' life.

For example, look at the first miracle related in the Book of John. This is the turning of the water into wine at the wedding in Cana. Weddings are a time of great joy.

It seems to me that in this miracle Jesus is affirming the importance of joy, festivity, and therefore laughter in human life. With this miracle Jesus is adding to the merriment of a happy celebration.

Or consider the story of the Prodigal Son. When a young man who has squandered his inheritance in a far-away land returns home, his father forgives him and throws a big party, "with singing and dancing." This time with a parable instead of a miracle, Jesus seems to me to be saying *"Yes!"* to the appropriateness of joy and laughter in human life.

Another way to consider humor in the Christian life is to think about it in relation to some of the main themes of the Bible. Consider, for example, Jesus' commandment to "Love one another."

I think that humor can have a very positive value in helping us to love each other. I have seen a number of times in my own experience where humor has greatly helped to de-fuse anger. I know that, over the years in Sally's and my marriage, we have been in arguments that have abruptly dissolved because something funny happened in the midst of our anger. And once we have shared a laugh, the mood of anger is broken.

Of course, it is also true that laughter can be used for very vicious and cruel purposes. But it is a wonderful fact that when laughter is properly used, it can have a very healing and holy effect in our human relationships with one another.

Another important theme in the Bible is the danger that comes from the sin of pride. It seems to me that a sense of humor can be one of the best weapons against pride. If we can look at our own foibles, mistakes and foolishness, and laugh at them, then that laughter can help keep us from getting carried away with arrogance and pride.

So I believe that humor is a wonderful gift from God and can greatly nourish our life of Christian faith. Sometimes humor can help us in our relationships with other people and ourselves. Other times humor serves to bring joy and laughter into our lives. And that is important too.

In fact, it's The Cat's Pajamas!

6

What Happened Next

As I sit writing these words, Mehitabel is dead.

It is impossible to believe.

People always say that cats have nine lives, and they seem to. Cats are so quick-footed they seem capable of endlessly eluding danger. And they heal so rapidly from injury that they appear to have limitless powers of regeneration.

But it doesn't go on forever. Nine is a finite number. There is always a tenth trial, but there isn't a tenth life.

Mehitabel had had a number of narrow escapes before. Twice she arrived at the back door with long, extremely deep gashes in her skin. We took her to the vet, got her stitched up, and she healed quickly.

Two other times we noticed infected cuts on Mehitabel's head. They turned out to be abscesses. Each time the vet lanced the wound, cleaned it out, and gave Mehitabel antibiotics. Each time she recovered beautifully.

But Mehitabel's final illness was more insidious. It took place gradually over several weeks time. It started in the early spring. Sally and I were coming up to the anniversary of our moving into the house (late May), and I was figuring out how long we had lived here. It turned out to be eleven years!

But then, with a start, I realized something else. If we have lived on Dorothy Street for eleven years, and Mehitabel was full-grown when we moved in, then that meant that she had to be a *minimum* of twelve years old. More likely, even older. It was the first time I realized that Mehitabel was an old cat. It was a strange and surprising thought.

Soon after that she began drinking a great deal of water during the daytime, something she had never done before. Then one weekend her weight dropped drastically. At first I tried to feed her something, but she wouldn't eat. Not even liver, her favorite. As soon as I saw that she wasn't interested in liver, I knew the end was at hand.

I made an appointment with the vet, but I hated doing it. Because I knew that Mehitabel would never be coming home.

The night before I took her in I sat up late in my reclining chair with her on my lap. She was extremely thin, but she was purring. Memories of the last ten years flooded through my mind: the jokes, the funny names, the fun times, all the funny places where she used to lie around the house, the companionship, the interesting thoughts she led me to, the constant delight she brought, the hugs in the night.

What an amazing and wonderful ten years!

The next day I took her to the vet.

When I called the animal hospital the day after, to find out the results of the tests, the doctor confirmed the worst. Mehitabel's kidneys had undergone a drastic irreversible collapse. I agreed to let the veterinarian give her a terminal injection.

I picked Sally up from work that afternoon, and we went to see Mehitabel one last time.

It was very difficult. We could hear her crying when we got to the vet's. We went back where all the animals were and found Mehitabel's cage. I opened the door and picked her up, and Sally and I both held her for the last time. We cried and Mehitabel purred. Then Sally and I went home.

So Mehitabel, my constant companion, best buddy, and wonderful friend is dead.

It seems so strange.

I go out into the back yard, and it seems empty now. Mehitabel enjoyed the back yard so completely, and loved it so much, that she *defined* it. It is as though the back yard had a very definite purpose, which is not being fulfilled now. I look at all Mehitabel's favorite places in the back yard, all the different places she used to sleep, or sun herself, or cool off, or explore. I look at all her favorite places on the sidewalk. They are all empty. I can't see what is there; all I can think of is what *isn't* there.

At night I wake up from my sleep with a start, thinking I hear a cat. But there is no cat.

Life and death.

It seems so strange, so incomprehensible. A thousand questions come into my mind. What happens when we die? Is Mehitabel alive as a spirit? What *is* a spirit? What lies beyond this life? What happens to *me* after this life?

I keep wondering about Heaven. What could Heaven possibly be like? It is an unknown land that shimmers out-of-focus in the distance.

I read the Bible.

Jesus' disciples ask him about Heaven. He describes it by saying, "In my Father's house there are many mansions." But I still wonder to myself, "What is Heaven really *like*?" I can't visualize it. I can't comprehend it.

I realize more then ever the necessity for faith. Truth is so strange, and mysterious, and lies so far beyond our understanding, that we can only reach it by faith.

One of my questions is this: In God's Heavenly Kingdom, filled as it is with many mansions, will a gray tabby cat ever come scratching at the door, asking to be let in?

I think of my days with Mehitabel with great nostalgia. I can see them so clearly. One scene in particular keeps running through my mind…

It is summer. I get up from the typewriter and walk out to the back yard, to mull over a word or phrase.

The leaves of the plants are an amazing green. They seem almost drunk on sunlight. I stop to look and listen.

The flowers on the hedge are voluptuous with pollen, and the back yard is filled with the subliminal hum of bees.

A turtle dove coos from the nearby telephone wires.

I see a white butterfly flutter through the air.

Mehitabel is lying on her side, in sensual luxury, underneath the shady fig tree. I go over, kneel down, and pet her and talk to her.

A thought occurs to me, and I start back into the house…

Wonderful days!

The summer days that will never end.

But they do end. Dorothy Street, like the summer, is only a season. The pressures for change have been building.

One pressure comes from my work situation. I have had a number of interesting assignments during the past several years, but they haven't ultimately turned out well for me. I have primarily been writing humorous, short videos for businesses and schools. They have won a number of awards but I haven't done very well from them financially. I need to make a major change, to find a completely different way to put things together. I need to find a whole new direction.

And there is the matter of the house. The house itself is getting more and more run-down, but because it is in a desirable area of the city, the rent is going sky high. We need to find some place else to live.

So the pressures for change, the pressures to move, have been building.

Then Mehitabel died.

For me Mehitabel *was* Dorothy Street. She is the central, focal symbol of those wonderful years. With Mehitabel dead it is the end of a way of life. It is the end of an era.

It's time to move on.

What lies ahead?

It is a mystery.

My life enters a time of change. But of course it's been changing all along, and it was during the time on Dorothy Street that I made the greatest change of my life. I became a Christian.

Accepting Jesus as my Lord and Savior is "The Great Change," because it affects all other changes.

What does it mean to be a Christian? Where does my Christian life lead me?

I ask myself these questions again and again with ever deepening answers.

I read the Bible and pray, in order to grow in faith and understanding.

The more I read the Bible, the more deeply I feel the overpowering truth of the Bible. The more I pray, the more strongly I feel the transforming power of prayer. The more I believe, the more I find that I am capable of belief.

So I enter a time of changes guided by the Holy Spirit.

What lies ahead?

Saint Paul once wrote, "Because of all I have *seen*, I have faith in all that I have *not* seen."

I look at my own life, at all the things I have seen since that long-ago Easter Sunday when I experienced my own resurrection from death to life. I have seen wonderful things. There have been disappointments and frustrations along the way. But these last years have been a time of great joy and wondrous blessings. And weaving through them all, unsought and unimagined, was Mehitabel, The Gift Cat.

I believe that God takes the material of each of our lives, and uses it to fashion parables of his kingdom, if we can but see them. One of the parables of my own life is Mehitabel. She is a parable of love, risk, change, and laughter. She is a parable of God's creation. But more than anything, Mehitabel is a parable of the fact that God moves through our lives with love and mystery, and brings us wonderful surprises, far greater than anything we could ever hope for or imagine.

What lies ahead?

Trust in the Lord!

END PART ONE

Part Two

7

The Time in the Desert

Twenty years have now passed since Sally and I moved away from Dorothy Street. It was a very difficult move because Dorothy Street had been the setting for so many wonderful things in my life.

It was on Dorothy Street that I first learned to love a cat. And it was on Dorothy Street that I first began to open my life to the enormous mystery and love of God. I continue to marvel at the way these two seemingly dissimilar adventures were intertwined, and how each one illustrated the other.

But Mehitabel was now dead, and we were now gone from Dorothy Street. I felt a little like Adam, being banished from the Garden of Eden. And indeed, the move ushered in a kind of personal "time in the desert" for me. It was a time when nothing seemed to work out quite right. It was a time of testing.

The house we moved into was in Sherman Oaks in the San Fernando Valley. It wasn't a bad move really, although the house was too small and never quite felt like home.

Since free lance jobs are often so hard to put together, I decided to find a corporate communications job on a staff somewhere. After sending out some applications, I found a good position with a financial institution and began working with great enthusiasm. But two years later I was fired. It was an extremely painful experience.

It was very hard to look for another job after that, but I did, and I was lucky enough to find a very good job in corporate communications with a utility company. It involved a long commute, but I was happy to have the job. Unfortunately this job lasted an even shorter period of time before I was fired.

Both of these jobs looked very good on paper. The main requirement in both of them was having good skills in language and communication, which is where all my experience has been. But the jobs also required a high degree of organization and ability with details. I have always had a great deal of difficulty in both of these areas, so it was almost inevitable that the jobs wouldn't work out well. But being fired from two jobs was a devastating experience. It gave me a feeling of extreme personal failure, and it was hard to shake.

And then there were cats.

Not long after we moved to the Valley, a friend who works at UCLA (where Sally also works) found a cat that had been abandoned on the campus. Sally heard about the cat and brought it home. It was black and white and was very young, scarcely more than a kitten. We named her Gracie. She was a very sweet cat, but the problem for me was that I was still grieving for Mehitabel. I never really bonded with Gracie.

Then one day she seemed very listless and had an odd look about her. We took her to the vet, who suggested that we leave her overnight while he ran some tests. We left Gracie and the vet called a couple of hours later to say that she had died! It was extremely shocking. The only thing I could figure out was that she had been bitten by a poisonous spider, or had possibly eaten some poison a neighbor left out for mice or the neighborhood possums.

So before we fully got used to her, Gracie was gone.

Then we moved again.

A friend who lived just a few blocks away decided to take a job in Northern California. Her house was one we had been in a number of times and liked. Also, it had more room. So, when she left to go up north, we moved in.

Like the house on Dorothy Street, this house also came with a cat. It was an old family cat named Sue that our friend Pat had had for many years. In fact Sue was *twenty*. That meant that, if every year of a cat's life equals five of ours, Sue was *100!* And she looked it. She was a calico cat and was extremely thin and frail. Obviously at that age and in that condition Sue couldn't possibly make a strenuous move. So our friend Pat moved on and Sue stayed behind in our care.

I was very happy because Sue and I fell in love. She was really a wonderful cat. Whenever I walked around the backyard, Sue would always follow along by my side. And when I sat down on the patio, she would jump up in my lap. Sue was really just scruffy fur and bones at this point in her life, but she was very loving and had a great spirit.

It was not a surprise when she finally died six months later. In fact, it seemed like a miracle she lasted that long. Amazingly she was still able to jump up on the wall in the back yard until a couple of weeks before she died. But she was so extremely old when I first met her that I didn't really grieve when she died. I just counted every day that I lived around her as a marvelous gift.

Her time in my life was like a meteor. She was a brief blaze that passed through quickly, lasting only a few moments, and then she was gone.

Not long after that our friend Mary called. She sounded desperate.

She and her husband had just moved into an apartment after several houses. Their cat Charlotte had always been used to being an indoor/outdoor cat. But now, the circumstances of their apartment forced them to keep Charlotte in all the time. Charlotte was miserable and kept meowing constantly. They needed to place her somewhere else. Quickly! Otherwise, she'd have to go to the pound, which they couldn't bear to think of. Was there any possibility *we* could take Charlotte?

"Yes." I said. "We'll be happy to take her."

So Charlotte became a member of the Evans household. She was a very sweet cat and we enjoyed having her around. However, she was not a kitten. In fact, she was fourteen. So we knew that we wouldn't be having a long life together. Then, just as we were starting to get used to her, the infamous Northridge Earthquake hit.

Our house itself wasn't seriously damaged, but the inside looked as though some giant had lifted the house up into the air, had violently shaken it back and forth a few times, and then put it back down on its foundation. Objects were flung across the rooms, the grandfather clock was knocked to the floor, glassware was thrown out of the cupboards and smashed against the walls, and the bottles and jars flew out of the refrigerator and spilled all over the linoleum floor. There was broken glass everywhere.

I'm not sure exactly what happened to Charlotte during the quake, but she was massively traumatized. She refused to come out from under the bed after that for any reason, and she stopped eating altogether. We took her to the vet and he tried a few things, but nothing worked. Two weeks later she was dead.

So the few years after moving from Dorothy Street were frustrating and perplexing. It was a time in the desert.

On Dorothy Street I discovered what a wonderful blessing and parable of God's love a cat could be. But then once I realized how much I could love a cat, I couldn't seem to keep one. And, although I had been praying for direction in my work situation, I got two jobs that I was fired from. The experience with the jobs was extremely painful and discouraging.

Did I still have faith? Well, yes, but it was very fragile. It felt like a spider web that the wind was insistantly tugging at. And I realized at this point in my life that the thing I needed to pray for most was faith itself.

8

Mental Images

In a dry season of perplexity and frustration, I found that my mind often drifted back to memories of happier times. And Mehitabel was central to many of them. Some of the memories from that time are warm and idyllic, like quiet evenings when Sally and I would be sitting in the living room at night, by a crackling fire, reading or talking, with Mehitabel on one of our laps.

Some of the memories from that time are funny.

Mehitabel used to do something that I called "the walk-through." She would meow at the back door to come in. I would go over and open the door for her. Then, once inside, she would walk slowly, regally, purposefully toward the *front* door and meow to go out! It wasn't that she changed her mind once inside. It was that *she came in for the purpose of going out the front door*.

Why, one might ask, would a cat do such a strange thing? Well, that is one of Life's Great Cat Questions.

When Mehitabel did her periodic "walk-throughs," she did them with an enormous sense of self-possession. The Queen of England at her coronation ceremony couldn't have walked down the aisle at Westminster Abbey with greater dignity than Mehitabel during her walk-throughs.

Back in the seventies, there was a cartoonist B. Kliban who exploded onto the national scene with an extravaganza of cat cartoons. He put out several books of cat drawings. He also had calendars, coffee mugs, and T-shirts. I got them all. They were very funny and quite brilliant. The great thing for me about Kliban's cartoons was that, with just a few deft lines, he caught the real comical *essence* of cats.

Once, when one of his books was published, there was a big promotional campaign, and my favorite bookstore had a five-foot-high cardboard representation of one of his cat cartoons. It was orange and black, with traces of white, and was standing on a display table. I was stunned when I first saw it because it was so funny and huge.

After the promotion, I asked the bookstore people if I could have the cat and they gave it to me. So I went home with the five-foot tall cardboard cat and put it on the floor of the living room. The pose of the cartoon shows the cat, sitting down, and looking out at the viewer.

One morning I walked into the living room, and there to my surprise I saw Mehitabel right in front of the Kliban cat, *seated in exactly the same pose as the giant cartoon cat behind her!* What an image! I laughed out loud when I saw it. And now, years later, I still laugh.

Not long after Mehitabel joined the Evans household, we became aware of a very interesting activity of hers: catching mice. Every month or so she would arrive at the back door uttering a strange-sounding meow, and when we looked to see what was happening, we could see that she had a mouse in her mouth. Often the mouse would still be alive. Our challenge was to keep her from bringing the mouse inside.

It was during these episodes that we learned first-hand about the often-talked-about game of "Cat and Mouse."

What we discovered is that it really *is* a game. At least it is for the cat. Not so much for the mouse.

Mehitabel would bring the mouse to the back door to present it to us. (And, after many mouse episodes, I really do believe that she *was* bringing it as a gift.) Then after she showed us the mouse, *she would let the mouse go*. The mouse would start to walk or run away, and might even get several feet. But then Mehitabel would run after the mouse and catch it all over again! This was a great sport for her.

She would often let the mouse go and re-catch it several times before she eventually ate it. After a few rounds of this, all the mouse could do would be to stagger along, dazed, not quite sure where it was going. It was certainly a dangerous game for the mouse. But it also had some risks for Mehitabel.

She always wanted the mouse to get a little ways away, but not so far away that she couldn't re-catch it. And every once in a while she miscalculated.

Once she caught a mouse near the garage. She let it go and caught it again. Then she let it go a *second* time, but this time the mouse abruptly changed direction, hurried over to a pile of boards, disappeared into a tiny crack, popped out the other end, and then scooted under the garage. He was *gone*!

Mehitabel couldn't believe it. She kept inspecting and re-inspecting the area, stalking back and forth, sniffing every possible entry or exit. And waiting… But the mouse never re-appeared. At that point he was probably deep in a burrow somewhere, regaling his mouse comrades with the saga of his heroic encounter with the ferocious giant cat, and how he escaped to tell the tale.

Another game of cat and mouse took place once on the patio. But, like the side of the garage, this area too had a complicated and irregular field. There were two chairs, a table, and a number of potted plants scattered around on three sides. Mehitabel was in the center with the mouse in her mouth.

She released it onto the cement and he just stood frozen for a moment before he started to trot toward the pots. Before the mouse reached them, Mehitabel pounced on him and grabbed him up. Then she released him again.

He was slow the first time, but the second time he was *fast*. He darted off toward a different pot, scrambled up the side, and scurried up the stem of the plant to the safety of a big, thick, horizontal, philodendron leaf almost as big as a dinner plate. He was standing on the leaf, safe, almost three feet above the ground. Mehitabel ran over to the pot, got up on her back legs and reached her right front paw up as high as she could. But no matter how much she stretched and strained, she was still about an inch short of the leaf where the mouse was perched.

It was an amazing sight, with the potted plant and its bright green leaf with the tiny gray mouse standing on top of it, just beyond the reach of the big gray cat that was desperately trying to grab it. What a frustrated cat, and what a funny sight!

So, after the move from Dorothy Street, when so many things in my own life seemed uncertain and perplexing, it was a tonic to remember some of the fun and funny things connected with Mehitabel. It is important to say here, though, that not everything connected with Mehitabel was pleasant or fun. For example, the times we had to take her to the vet.

In the eleven or so years that we had her we probably took her to the vet seven or eight times. But each time was a horrible trauma for everyone concerned (except for the vet). In order to get Mehitabel over there, we had to put her in a carrying box. But it was a Herculean task to get her in.

She struggled and fought mightily. It took both Sally and me using all our concentration and strength (and wiles!). And if we didn't get her in quickly enough, she would run under the bed where she knew we couldn't reach her. It was just a horrible, exhausting experience. I don't know who hated it more, me or Mehitabel.

And the experience didn't always end at the vet's. Often the vet would give us a packet of pills to give Mehitabel once or twice a day. And Mehitabel hated taking pills! It *could* have been very easy, but in fact it wasn't, because Mehitabel struggled and fought against it so much.

During the time on Dorothy Street I used to have a green rug by my side of the bed. It was about four feet long, bright green, and in the shape of a footprint. It came from a Jolly Green Giant promotion.

Once, during a visit to the vet, he gave us some antibiotic pills for Mehitabel. We were supposed to give her one every day. The problem was it was almost impossible to get her to swallow them because she struggled so much. One time I eventually did get a pill down her after several difficult, unpleasant tries. Neither one of us was happy after the episode.

Later that day I went into the bedroom and had to laugh out loud. Because right in the middle of the bright green footprint rug was a B. M.! Mehitabel was showing me how angry she was at me for forcing the pill down her throat.

I have often reflected about Mehitabel and the parable of her resistance to going to the vet and taking her pills. In all those instances she had some kind of serious injury. She was in pain and needed healing. What she needed *most* was to get medical treatment. But she struggled against it. She was afraid. She fought against the very thing she needed to do to become healed. How ironic.

Actually though, that sounds a lot like the rest of us, doesn't it?

Most of the memories I have of Mehitabel involve her *doing* something, like sitting on boxes, or doing a "walk-through," or catching mice. And there are endless funny images I have of her, like the time I saw her in front of the giant cartoon cat. But one of the things that always fascinated me about Mehitabel was her ability to do *nothing*.

Cats sleep a lot and Mehitabel certainly did, too. But there was something else she did that seemed similar, but I believe was quite different. She would lie down somewhere and seem to mentally "gather herself in." Then she would enter a state of deep quietness. It almost looked as though she was meditating. That is what I mean by "doing nothing." It seemed to be a very positive state.

And the ability to "do nothing" in the sense that I am speaking *is* an ability. Seeing Mehitabel enter that quiet state so easily and so often makes me realize how *un*-quiet we twenty-first century human beings are. With our Blackberries, Palm Pilots and cell phones we are constantly "on call" and lead an agitated existence. I have several times seen men in rest rooms, talking on cell phones while they are using the urinal. Good grief!

Our biological natures could teach us something. The heart is programmed to have significant quiet time. It beats; it rests; it beats; it rests. But we contemporary humans are trying to circumvent that. We live systolic lives and try to suppress our diastolic needs.

As Christians we are certainly called to be productive and be good stewards of the time and talents God has given us. But, like the ancient Israelites, we are also given the gift and the command of the Sabbath. Our sin is that we no longer honor the Sabbath or rest in it. It is now just a day to catch up on the work we missed during our multi-tasking week days.

Jesus came into the world as the "Prince of Peace." We most often think of that peace as being peace between individuals and groups. The peace that comes from loving one another. He certainly calls us to this peace.

But there is also another kind of peace: the peace within an individual's mind and heart. This individual inner peace is both a gift and a command. It is a gift to believers that comes from the Holy Spirit. But it is also a command that Jesus gives us. He tells us in The Sermon on the Mount (Matthew 6) not to worry. And in the Parable of the Sower (Luke 8) he warns us that if we worry, we are in danger of losing the Kingdom. Worry robs us of our inner peace.

So, with Mehitabel I have seen a small furry model of someone living with great peace and quietness of spirit. It is a little nudge that reminds me that it is possible to live with peace. And it reminds me that in an unquiet age it is important for all of us to worry less and find intentional strategies to bring greater peace into our lives.

Maybe what we need to do is take purring lessons from cats.

9

Work it Out

When I had my dramatic encounter with God on that long ago Easter Sunday, there were six words that were emblazoned on my mind and heart. They were, "You belong here. Work it out."

During those first years, "working it out" was easy. It almost happened automatically. My understanding seemed to increase daily, new ideas tumbled out constantly, God informed my dreams at night, scripture spoke directly to every question and need. And always Mehitabel was there, providing the perfect illustration for every spiritual truth. It was an immensely joyful time. I realize now that it was my honeymoon with God.

Then it all ended.

Just as my personal life changed with the death of Mehitabel, the move, and the job problems, my spiritual life also changed. I still felt under the injunction to "work it out," but now it was a struggle. The emphasis now seemed to be on "work," and I wasn't sure how to do it. I was active in church all this time, but church has never been the primary focus of my spiritual life.

However favorable my outward circumstances may have looked, inwardly I felt completely adrift. I was still praying frequently, but now my prayers were really cries for help: "Lord, where am I supposed to go? What do I do *now*?! Lord, **help**!"

It wasn't until much later that I realized that what I was going through wasn't that unusual. In fact, the Psalms are filled with very similar cries for help. They contain all kinds of different moods and topics, including praise and thanksgiving, but again and again they also contain painful cries from the heart. "My soul is in anguish. How long, O Lord, how long?" (Psalm 6:3). "Why, O Lord, do you stand far off? Why do you hide yourself in times of trouble?" (Psalm 10:1).

It is amazing to me to realize that these Psalms were written by the man who was the **King of Israel**! *I* struggle along with pain and uncertainly, but I'm just an ordinary person. *David* was anointed by God to lead his favored nation. He was beloved by God and was given miraculous victories as a leader in battle, and also single-handedly in his contest with Goliath. And it was David's line that God chose for the eventual incarnation of the Messiah. David was God's personal hero. How could someone so favored by God possibly suffer doubt and discouragement?

The reality, I think, is that God tests us all. He withholds his blessings periodically from all of us, sometimes for long periods of time, to determine our faith and commitment. I believe it is important to him to see if we're truly on board. Or, during all those times that we're professing our love for him, are we really just looking over God's shoulder, scanning the crowd to see if there's somebody else at the party who might be more interesting.

I wondered about some of the great Christian leaders and teachers through history, like St. Augustine, St. John of the Cross, Dietrich Bonhoffer, Dorothy Day, Henri Nouwen. How had they handled their fears and uncertainties? What had they done during times when God seemed absent?

I began reading their works and biographies and found them to be a great treasure. Along the way I ran across a rather recent book by Richard Foster that was especially helpful. The book is titled, *Celebration of Discipline.* It is about the Christian disciplines, those specific activities we can practice to deepen our relationship with God.

There are several traditional Christian disciplines, and a couple of them, like Bible reading and prayer, are quite familiar. But there are others that aren't so familiar. One of them struck me as being particularly interesting. It was something I had never even thought about before. It was the practice of the discipline of *silence.*

The first time I tried to be silent was at a retreat led by Richard Foster. He guided the whole group in a day of silence, during which we wandered around the grounds of the retreat center and wrote our thoughts in a journal. It felt strange and uncomfortable to be silent for a day. I realized later that my problem was that I'd been *poking* and *prodding* at the silence, instead of *resting* in it.

But I was still intrigued enough by the idea of silence to try it again. The second time was at a Benedictine abbey in the high desert north of Los Angeles. St. Andrew's Abbey is a real monastery with resident monks. But there are also some very plain cabins for visitors, and both monks and visitors eat at the same time in the dining hall. I pinned a small sign on my shirt to let people know I was on a personal, silent retreat.

My second time in silence was much more successful than the first. I got more into the rhythm of it this time, and began to see that the spiritual discipline of silence is really about *listening* to God. We all tend to lead noisy lives, where we're talking most of the time. And we're often even noisy in prayer, because we're *talking* to God. But silence gives us a chance to listen to God and receive the thoughts and guidance he has for us.

At the time of this writing I have been going on three-day personal, silent retreats for over a dozen years. I find it a time I always look forward to and enjoy tremendously. And out of the silence I almost always gain some kind of insight, guidance, or even a surprising new thought or revelation. It is a time during which I often feel a great closeness to God.

One of the things I have come to realize about prayer is that it not only has an effect on the person or situation prayed for, but also has an effect on the person praying. It changes us. Over time, prayer takes the elements of our lives and thought and begins to fashion something new. New themes and concerns begin to emerge in our lives. Prayer is a kind of spiritual photosynthesis.

One of the things I believe prayer led me to several years ago was a strong desire to bring people together. It seemed to me that everywhere I looked I saw a world of people at odds with each other. We humans are fractured along fault lines of race, class, ethnicity, faith, age, gender and culture. I wanted to help bring people together. But how?

An answer first came after the civil unrest that followed the Rodney King beating. The white church I belonged to began some tentative interactions with an African-American church in the same denomination (Presbyterian). When the director of the Gospel choir in the other church learned of my enthusiasm for jazz, he invited me to sing in their choir. I showed up for their next rehearsal and never looked back.

I ended up spending over ten years in the Gospel choir of the African-American church, and it was one of the most extraordinary times in my life. What a glorious celebration Gospel music is! The psalms tell us to "make a joyful noise," and the Gospel choir certainly did. The choir also provided a wonderful setting for a helpful and healing dialogue about race. It was a great opportunity to help bring people together. Hallelujah!

Another opportunity to help bring people together came about in a strange and unlikely way.

I heard about a multiethnic group that was forming for the purpose of developing conflict resolution skills. They planned to use those skills to mediate interethnic disputes in Los Angeles. The training period was scheduled to last for two years. I signed up.

Looking back on it I'm not quite sure why I did. I was attracted to the fact that the group was multiethnic. But I was very uncomfortable with the idea of being a mediator. In fact, there was not once during the entire two years of training that I ever felt I would actually be acting as a mediator. I felt extremely ill at ease during all the many role-plays we engaged in.

So why did I continue with the training? I'm truthfully not sure. The real thing that kept me there was a strong sense that, although I couldn't explain it, I was "supposed to be there."

At the end of two years I received my mediation certification. Shortly after that the members of our class had an opportunity to serve as volunteer mediators in an alternative dispute resolution program in the local court system. I decided to do a couple of mediations just to round out the two-year experience. It would bring some closure and then I could move on. So I signed up.

I handled my first two cases very awkwardly. I felt so much pressure to be certain the paper work was done right, that I hardly paid any attention to the disputants. In spite of that I decided to try another couple of cases. They were only slightly better.

But by the time I got to the fifth case, everything changed. Something clicked. I was completely at ease in the role of mediator. I felt strong. It was as though I was born to do this work and had finally arrived at my destiny.

It still amazes me how natural and comfortable I feel when mediating, and yet how little inkling I had along the way that I would. I have now done over 400 mediations and currently work as a professional mediator in my own private practice. I continued to work part time in the court program for a while, and in both 2000 and 2001 I received *Outstanding Case Awards* from the Los Angeles County Board of Supervisors.

I have a tremendous passion for mediation, and at this point I've worked with a huge variety of cases: couples splitting up, business conflicts, neighborhood and real estate disagreements, family and custody issues, organization problems, and contract disputes. Several have included acts of violence.

One of my cases involved a 94-year old woman suing her 72-year old daughter, because she believed the daughter had stolen the rights to her burial crypt. There were seven family members present for the mediation, and they represented three generations. Two of the family members even flew in from out of state. It turned out that they had a number of other conflicts beyond the initial one, and I ended up working with that family for over a year.

In another case one of the parties was a top official in the Teamsters Union. He came to the mediation with two body-guards.

Still another time I was mediating a dispute between two estranged brothers, who were arguing over the inheritance from their deceased parents. The amount of money in question was slightly over one million dollars. One of the brothers, the one who had initiated the mediation, told me privately at one point that he would be willing to overlook the entire amount of money, if his brother would just apologize to him. The amazing power of an apology! For this brother an apology was literally worth a million dollars.

I believe one of the most important things a mediator can bring to any conflict situation is **hope.** People involved in a conflict are usually caught up in a swirl of negative emotions: anger, fear, discouragement, powerlessness, pain, and loss. And they often have an overwhelming feeling of being trapped in the conflict. They've tried every possibility, explored every option, and nothing has worked. They're stuck with nowhere to go.

They need the gift of hope. I myself always feel profoundly hopeful when I'm dealing with people in conflict. And ironically, sometimes the more troubled a case is, the more hopeful I feel. Some of that comes from my temperament I think. But my real reason for hope comes from my faith.

I don't necessarily talk about my faith with the parties involved in mediation, especially when I work in the court system. But inwardly I always call on God to be present and guide all my work. There is a great power and peace that comes from the knowledge of his presence. Jesus has called us to "Love One Another" and he is available to help us. He offers the gift of his Holy Spirit. He wants *all* of our relationships to be transformed and whole.

Another reason I feel hope comes from the experiences I have had. I have done hundreds of mediations now and I am constantly amazed at how they turn out. There are unexpected twists and turns, surprises, and resolutions I would never have predicted. They often seem truly miraculous. As a result of witnessing so many unlikely outcomes, there are two principles that have emerged for me, and they guide all my thinking.

The principles are these:

- **Wherever we are right now is not necessarily where we're going to end up**. And…
- **There is *always* something we can do.**

I think about these two principles all the time. At this point they are practically in my DNA. And the more experiences I have, the more strongly I believe them.

Here's what happens:

People in a conflict often have a hard time seeing beyond the conflict. To the parties involved, it often feels like the conflict is an end point.

But what people don't realize is that the impasse they're in, however frustrating and "final" it seems, is really *just one point along the way.* It seems like the end, but it isn't. Everything is in process. There are always many factors at work, some quite surprising, and there is no telling what direction things will go. I have witnessed the truth of this principle again and again: **Wherever we are right now is not necessarily where we're going to end up!**

And **there is always something we can do.** There are a variety of tools and resources we can always use. It seems almost endless. One of the techniques I use most often is *re-framing.* Re-framing is just a simple matter of approaching a problem from a different angle, or looking at it through another kind of lens, or maybe asking a new question we hadn't asked before. Re-framing is a powerful tool. Often a problem that seems totally resistant becomes very easy to solve once we re-frame it and look at it from a different perspective.

There is always something we can do!

So for several years now I have been following the injunction of the Holy Spirit that long-ago Easter morning to "work it out." The process of "working it out" has been an amazing journey that has led me into Gospel singing, into silence, and into the art of conflict resolution.

As I have proceeded on this journey I have come to believe that *each one of us, as a believer or disciple, is called to some kind of personal ministry*. By ministry I mean simply taking the gifts and talents God has given us, and using those gifts in his service.

The most obvious kind of ministry, of course, is being a pastor of a church. But that's just one kind of ministry. I believe we are *all* called to ministry. It is not an option. And there is a wide variety of different kinds of possible ministries, just as there is an enormous variety of different kinds of people.

Each one of us is created and equipped for some kind of ministry, based on our individual talents, temperament, circumstances and spiritual gifts. It is up to each one of us to discover the ministry that God has created us for, and to consecrate ourselves to his service through that ministry. It is a wonderful adventure to discover what it is.

In that sense we're *all* "working it out."

I believe one of the primary ministries God has called me to and equipped me for is working with people in conflict, and bringing them the gift of hope and transformation. This is my own personal ministry and it brings me an immense amount of joy.

10

A Real Life Story

Out of several hundred mediations I have been involved in, I have had many wonderful experiences. The following is the true story of one of them. I call it:

War and Peace

Right from the start the situation was explosive. The scene was a mediation session between two angry families whose backyards are separated by a low fence. The conference room was very small, but there were ten people present: Two single mothers, who were the heads of their households, along with children of various ages, from a grown daughter and teen-agers, all the way down to a baby in arms. It started out noisy and it got noisier.

The families had gotten along quite well when they first became neighbors two years before. They often went back and forth between houses. But then tension started to build, and before long it erupted into violence. One day one of the mothers, Regina McGibbon (real names not used), jumped out of her car and started to strangle thirteen year old Ronnie Jones. (She later said she was only trying to "scare" him and "teach him a lesson.") Another time, the oldest Jones boy grabbed one of the McGibbon girls by the hair, and swung her around in a circle. And they increasingly used language toward each other that was insulting and abusive.

The event that finally brought the two families to court was the vandalism of Regina McGibbon's new car. She went out one day and was shocked to discover a deep gash etched in the paint all the way around her car. Regina's two teen-age girls claimed they saw young Ronnie Jones climb over the fence, deliberately scratch the car, and then disappear back over the fence. So Regina McGibbon sued Ronnie's mother Lettie for $2,500 to repair the car. That's when I met them all. I was called in to mediate the case.

Ronnie heatedly denied scratching Regina's car. He accused Regina of getting the two girls to lie about him. He insisted he was innocent, and so did his mother and sister. We looked at police reports and heard everybody's testimony several times. It kept getting louder and angrier, and the mediation session continued for almost four hours.

Toward the end of that time I was standing out in the hall talking to Lettie. She seemed exhausted from all the emotion and stress. She said at that point that she just wanted to get the suit behind her, so she agreed to pay the $2,500. It wasn't an admission of anything. She was tired. She needed to move on.

So we went back inside and joined the others. I started to write up the agreement for Lettie to pay Regina. At this point all the noise and active hostility abruptly stopped. As I was working out the wording of the agreement, I said I thought we needed to add something. I said that there had been so much hurtful language used, and so many accusations back and forth (some very ugly, and far beyond the case at hand), that it would be good if they all apologized to each other. Just so they could all start afresh. They agreed. (I even wrote this into the agreement.) So we began to go around the circle with everyone apologizing. It ended up with Ronnie.

When it was his turn he took a long pause. Then he looked at Regina, and in a quiet voice, confessed that he had scratched her car. He apologized and asked her to forgive him. She said she would. It was an amazing moment. And once they had that exchange, there was a great sense of peace that came over the room.

One of Regina's children was a toddler. He had been quietly playing on the floor with his toys during the whole mediation. But now, as everyone prepared to leave the room, he was talking a mile a minute. Regina shook her head and said to me, "That's amazing! *He has never spoken before!* Only a few single words, but never a whole stream like this! I can't believe it." So the whole experience we had just gone through was liberating and transforming even for the toddler!

As they were all filing out, one of the girls who was about ten years old stopped and said to me, "Does this mean we're all friends now?"

I said, "Yes, it does. *But you'll have to keep working at it!* You'll have to be careful from now on not to use hurtful language, and you'll all have to be sure to treat each other with respect, just the way *you* would want to be treated."

And so they returned home, ready for a new beginning.

One of the hardest things for people to do is to admit they have done something wrong, and to apologize for it. But there are times when it happens, and when it does it is a wonderful and holy moment.

11

Moving Across the Street

My time on Dorothy Street with Mehitabel was quite extraordinary. It was a time filled with wonderful blessings, both personal and spiritual. Then when Mehitabel died and we moved, I felt a huge sense of loss. I tried to recapture the experience with another cat, but I couldn't seem to keep one for any length of time. I found it confusing and disappointing.

I resigned myself to the realization that I wouldn't be having another cat. The experience with Mehitabel was amazing and wonderful, but not repeatable. It was like Halley's Comet: a once in a lifetime event. And it helps me appreciate just how wondrous and fragile every moment and every experience truly is.

There were other cats in our new neighborhood in San Fernando Valley, of course, but they either belonged to somebody, or they were feral. The family that lived in the house on the corner directly across from us had three cats which we would see from time to time. Occasionally one would venture across to our front yard.

There were indications of serious trouble in that house. We would hear what sounded like arguments and drunken yelling. Then the father disappeared, and the family's tenure in the house finally ended with a dramatic episode involving the paramedics. In the last months before they left, one of their cats, a gray tabby, started coming over to our yard more and more frequently.

It seemed odd to me the way the cat behaved. I would walk outside to the car, or to get the paper, and the cat would be there, watching me intently. It wasn't a hostile look, or a challenging look. It was a very *interested* look.

When the family across the street finally moved out, the mother brought a U-haul, and she and the kids loaded up the last of their belongings and drove off. They took two of their cats with them: the white cat that was the mother's, and the black-and-white cat that was the daughter's. They left the gray tabby cat behind.

So the gray tabby cat moved over to our side of the street and it became official: she was now our cat. We named her Minnie.

It took me a while before I realized just what a wonderful cat Minnie really is. There was the inevitable shakedown cruise where we all needed to get used to each other. But I began to see what a sweet disposition she has, and how warm and affectionate she is. And although at first Minnie seemed skittish about sitting on Sally's or my lap, she quickly became a splendid lap cat. Before long it was like being with Mehitabel all over again.

Minnie has been with us now for seven years. They have been wonderful years!

Just like Mehitabel on Dorothy Street,the back yard is a wonderland for Minnie. Sometimes she is completely obvious, stretched out in sensual luxury in the very middle of the grass. Other times she is shrouded in secrecy. I may walk through the back yard calling for her and not get any response, not even have a hint that she's anywhere nearby. Then I turn back toward the house, and seconds after I arrive at the back door Minnie will mysteriously appear on the back steps.

Other times she will appropriate some unlikely spot she's never been before. One morning I walked out on the patio to discover Minnie sitting on the ladder! (This is the picture on the front cover of this book.) Luckily there was a camera nearby and I got the picture. I laugh every time I look at it. What was she doing on the ladder? I have no idea.

My relationship with Mehitabel, coming when and how it did, was very much of a parable to me. But in a very different way so is my experience with Minnie. It is to me a parable of the mystery of God's timing. When Mehitabel died I grieved for quite a while. After that I didn't actually *pray* for another cat but I certainly hoped for one. And it was extremely puzzling to me when I had so many false starts.

Finally I gave up. And that was when Minnie appeared. My experience with Minnie reminds me that God does respond to the hopes and prayers of those who love him. But it's always with *his* timing. God's oceanic patience constantly tests our own.

It is fascinating to me how similar Minnie and Mehitabel are, and yet how different. They both share that great core of mellow, purring catness. And they have the same color and markings: grey tabbies with circles on their sides. One of my favorite quotes, by Mark Twain, is: "History doesn't repeat itself, but it does *rhyme*." Minnie and Mehitabel definitely rhyme with each other.

There was one funny thing that Mehitabel used to do that Minnie now does too. Mehitabel would be walking along slowly beside Sally or me, and then would throw herself down on her side, **thump**! This was her signal that we were supposed to bend down and pet her. Which, of course, we did. We've always called it "fall-down-and-be-petted." It almost always happened on the gray Navajo rug in our living room.

Now, all these many years later, in different circumstances and a different cat, Minnie does exactly the same thing. Walk, walk, walk, walk, **thump**! And she also does it on the Navajo rug. Minnie and Mehitabel definitely do rhyme.

One of the things that *is* unique about Minnie is the way she looks at me. She started doing this when she lived across the street, but she still does it quite often. It seems very unusual to me for a cat to look at a person so directly. But as I mentioned, it's not in any way a challenging look, or a "facing down" kind of look. It's more of an *interested* look. It seems very affectionate, and it always accompanies very affectionate behavior. Actually it is wonderful.

One day a couple of years ago, I decided to go to the Abbey for a three-day silent retreat. But it just so happened that, during that same time, Sally was planning to go to Northern California for her annual get-together with one of her oldest friends from grade school. So I decided that, instead of going to the Abbey, I would have my silent retreat at home. The phone machine could take my messages, and I could return them later, just as I would if I were at the Abbey.

So I drove Sally to the airport. Then I returned home and began my silent retreat. In the first few hours Minnie was in and out a couple of times. Then the third time she came in she started meowing at me. She seemed upset over something, but I couldn't tell what it was. I looked at her water and food dishes and both were fine. But she still kept meowing. I couldn't figure it out. Then it finally hit me.

Most of the time I'm around Minnie I talk to her, and have for years. Now, all of a sudden I was silent, and not saying anything. Why? It puzzled Minnie and made her uneasy. So she meowed at me.

I reassured her by petting her. When I finally started talking again she was fine. But Minnie really didn't like the silent retreat!

My last birthday was one I was looking forward to, although by now it has reached an absurdly large number. My age is now starting to resemble the numbers astromoners use to describe distances between galaxies. But I was excited about my birthday nonetheless.

During the week before, Sally took me to a fabulous performance of Cirque de Soliel. That seemed to me to be the perfect gift for a birthday, because the acrobatics symbolize optimism, transcendence, and the possibility of the impossible.

Then the morning of my birthday I opened the back door and discovered another gift, this one from Minnie: a dead mouse on the doorstep!

I have had many wonderful birthday gifts over the years, but none quite as special as this. What is fascinating is that Minnie had brought "gifts" of mice before, but not very many, and none for quite a few months. But now one on my birthday!

This birthday was interesting in another way, because it had a theme. It was an unexpected theme that kept recurring again and again in a variety of different ways throughout the several days of my birthday season. The theme was faith.

It started with the Cirque de Soleil. A friend, who had seen the same performance Sally and I did, remarked that the teams of acrobats had to have absolute faith in each other. Then another friend unexpectedly shared an email article about faith. Faith also came up in other surprising ways in conversations. and two people sent greeting cards where faith was a key element.

Faith.

My birthday theme reminds me that I need to have faith. Faith that God loves us; faith that God is always there to guide us; faith that God sustains us even through times of pain; faith that God has created each one of us with a special and unique purpose; and faith that God has many blessings for us. One of those blessings might even be a wonderful cat, offering her birthday gift of a dead mouse.

12

God's Surprises

The Book of John states that "God is love." The Psalms speak of God as the architect of creation. Both views of God are profoundly apt. But for me personally, I often think of God as the *master of surprises*. God always surprises me.

He surprised me by reaching out in love and claiming me, even though I had angrily rejected him for so long. He surprised me by opening my mind and heart to a wonderful relationship with a cat, even though I had always hated cats before. He surprised me further by using my new relationship with Mehitabel as a parable of my on-going spiritual journey. He surprised me by guiding me to a second career that was completely unexpected, and yet one that perfectly uses all the skills and experience I developed earlier. And he surprised me by blessing me with a second gift cat, Minnie, after I'd given up hope of ever finding one.

God moves in our lives, and it's never the way we expect him to. He will *always* surprise us.

Almost every time I've been to the Abbey something has surprised me. And it almost always comes in a different way. Sometimes it's a passage of scripture; sometimes it's a dream; once very recently it came from a book, read aloud by one of the monks during dinner. And another time, not long ago, it came during a walk down a country road near the Abbey.

One of my greatest pleasures at the Abbey is taking long walks. Sometimes overhead I see pairs of hawks, hitching rides on wind currents, gliding impossible distances without a wing beat. Or I see a shiny black beetle, lumbering along through the dust by the road. At night there are thousands of stars strewn across the sky. I often hear them serenaded by a warty chorus of bullfrogs.

Recently I went up to the Abbey, determined to enjoy just such a walk. As I started driving north, clouds were gathering. When I arrived at the Abbey, I could clearly see they were rain clouds. By the time I checked in and got outside for my walk, there was a steady, gray drizzle. But I had a hat, a waterproof coat and a change of shoes. Nothing was going to stop me.

A couple of the main roads by the Abbey have blacktop, but my favorite road, one that makes a long ascent to the top of a hill, is nothing but dirt. That was the road I was determined to climb.

It was already starting to get muddy, so I kept my eyes focused on the road, to keep from slipping. But as I did so, I saw something I'd never seen before.

The Abbey is located in the high desert. There is vegetation all through the area, but it is very drab. Clumps of growth, two or three feet high, all about the same shade of earth brown. It is all very nondescript and invisible. I had walked past the vegetation on this road seventy or eighty times before, and I had never noticed it. But today, for the first time, I did.

With my eyes focused downward I now noticed a plant by the road. It was small and each branch had a row of tiny bells. I moved closer for a better look. It was quite beautiful. It had a look of delicate, fragile perfection, like a Japanese tea cup.

Then I noticed the plant next to it. It was totally different; overloaded with pollen, branches weighed down almost to the breaking point, hoarding the summer. You could almost hear it groan.

Two plants, side by side, a complete contrast in shape and image, but almost exactly the same color!

At this point I got fascinated and started looking at other plants near by. There was an amazing variety. I counted twenty-three different kinds. Plants that were thick, thin, bold, fuzzy, furry, feathery, spiky, and spidery. One had perfect round balls. Some were like centrifuges, with branches flung outward. Others were huddled close to the ground. One was like a garish French harlot, and one was like an Amish great aunt.

And all the plants were essentially the same color.

There was extravagant beauty by the side of the road. It was just a few feet away. I had passed by it countless times before. And I had completely missed it!

I have reflected upon this experience many times since then, and I find it very sobering. The question that occurs to me is this: If I am missing something so close and obvious as this, **what else am I missing?**

God's surprises. This is a surprise that has nudged me to become more open, more attentive, and (I hope) more aware of myself and of the world and people around me.

Sometimes, of course, the surprises in our lives are painful. They can fill us with immense sadness or loss. They can create what seem like insurmountable challenges.

I think of my friend Malcolm. In addition to being a good friend, Malcolm was also my first spiritual director. We got together frequently. At one point I took a full time job that was many miles away from where Malcolm lived. I was so consumed with the problems of work and travel that several months went by when I didn't see him, although we spoke several times on the phone. During that time Malcolm developed cancer of the pancreas.

When my schedule changed, I called and told him I would love to come by and say hello. I knew he was ill and couldn't get out easily. But I wasn't prepared for just *how* ill he was. His appearance was shocking.

Malcolm was sitting in his bed in light pajamas. He was hooked up to a bottle that was dripping fluid into his arm. I have never seen anyone before or since that was so thin. His arms and legs were not much thicker than a broom handle. It was hard to imagine how he was still alive.

And yet, as soon as I entered the room, he greeted me warmly and launched into an animated conversation. He seemed amazingly vigorous, and his mind was clear and insightful. We touched on a wide variety of topics. As always, we talked about spiritual matters, and Malcolm reflected aloud about the great mystery of his illness. He said the radiation and chemotherapy had been very difficult, and that he knew he wouldn't survive. In spite of that, he said, the illness had been a huge blessing for him.

He said he had had some personal problems that the illness forced him to deal with. He also said that he had grown much closer to God, and that ultimately the illness was one of the best things that had ever happened to him. He reminded me of the passage in Romans that says, "All things work for good for those who love the Lord."

Malcolm mentioned several books he thought I might like. Then he said he wanted to pray aloud for me. I left a short while later feeling very buoyed up. It was amazing. I had gone there to take cheer and encouragement to Malcolm, but I ended up receiving cheer and encouragement from him.

A week later Malcolm was dead.

I think of the strange surprises connected with Malcolm. First the devastating news of his fatal illness. But then the way he transformed it, turning a disaster into a blessing, not just for him, but also for me. These are surprises with enormous mystery at the heart of them.

Recently another friend, Steve, who was very young, died after a long and heroic struggle with cancer. My family has a long and wonderful history with his wife Peggi, because her grandfather, Frank Walkup, was a Presbyterian minister, and went to seminary with my father back in the nineteen twenties. I got to know Frank quite well when he moved into the same retirement community nearby, where my father lived the last years of his life.

When Steve died, Frank, his grandfather-in-law flew back for the memorial service from Florida, where he was then living. Frank was 92 years old and flew clear across the country from Florida to California with the help of one of his daughters.

I saw Frank at the reception after the memorial service and went over to talk to him. I knew that he was starting to have some problems with his memory, so I was careful to clearly establish who I was. I explained that I was Ralph Evans' son. He brightened when I said that and he began to reminisce about when he and my dad were in seminary together. He said that one of their classes together was on homiletics (preaching), and that he remembered hearing my dad preach his first sermon.

My dad's first sermon!

I happened to have heard dad's very *last* sermon, preached just a year or so before he died. So there Frank and I were, talking about dad's first and last sermons, bookends to a preaching career that spanned more than sixty years! It was an amazing experience.

Then Frank kind of cocked his head and looked at me like he was sizing me up. He asked me how tall I was. I was very surprised by the question and said I was around six one. (Frank at his age was considerably shorter.) He told me he had just received a pair of pajamas as a gift, but they were a little too large for him. He thought they would probably fit me. Would I like them? I said I would, so the next day at church his daughter gave me a package containing Frank's pajamas! (He had already flown back to Florida.)

Talk about God's surprises. Who would ever imagine that they would go to a memorial service and have a 92-year-old man offer them a pair of pajamas! I laugh every time I think about it. I treasure the pajamas and I marvel at that encounter with Frank. It was funny; it was deep; it was surprising; and it was mysterious. It seems to me to be very typical of the way God operates. God felt powerfully present.

It is now early morning. I am sitting on the patio drinking my first cup of coffee. The sun has sent a few tentative rays of light into the new day, like a wary swimmer, testing the water with a big toe, deciding whether or not to plunge in. I am starting to make some notes, preparing for a complex mediation in Orange County that will begin this afternoon. Sally has already left for the university, where she is leading a workshop today in her special area of Fulbright Fellowships. Minnie is still curled up on the bed, luxuriating in the dream world of cats.

I wore Frank's pajamas last night. I ration them and only wear them once in a while, because I don't want them to wear out. It is a wonderful experience to wear them.

They lift my mind upward, outward, inward, heavenward. I think of them as Cosmic Pajamas. God's Pajamas! They symbolize to me the surprising, mysterious, and sometimes funny ways that God constantly moves in all our lives.

I marvel at the surprises in my own life since first moving to Dorothy Street. The surprise of God's claiming me on my own personal resurrection Sunday. The parable of my wonderful Gift Cat, Mehitabel. My new career in conflict resolution. The plants at the Abbey. Malcolm. The pajamas. My other Gift Cat, Minnie. Amazing surprises all!

On that long-ago Easter Sunday, when my life changed forever, my instruction was to "work it out." I continue to try to "work it out" as I look ahead to God's next surprises. I am guided by scripture and transformed by prayer. I am blessed by a multitude of Holy Connections in community with God's other children. And when I go to the Abbey, I am spiritually nourished by encounters with God in the Great Cathedral of Silence.

What lies ahead?

Trust in the Lord!

About the Author

David Evans began his writing career in Cleveland, after college, writing funny greeting cards for American Greetings. He has written over 4,000 cards, including many bestsellers.

Later David moved to Los Angeles, where he worked as a comedy writer, winning an **EMMY Award** for writing on ***The Monkees***.

Drawing on his background as the son of a Presbyterian minister, he wrote **"THE GOOD BOOK... of Bible Cartoons,"** with drawings by long-time drawing partner Sherman Labby.

David has written about his spiritual journey in his book "**Does GOD Ever Speak Through CATS?"**

Another collaboration with drawing partner Sherman Labby is his graphic novel comedy adventure, **"The Hooper Brothers: Who's in Front?"**

In addition to humor, David is also an award-winning mediator. As part of his early mediation training David went to South Africa for a conflict resolution immersion experience, where he met with members of Archbishop Desmond Tutu's **Truth and Reconciliation Commission.**

For three years he served as a mediator for the **Los Angeles County Court Alternative Dispute Resolution Program**. At 16,000 cases a year it is the largest such program in the nation. For two of David's three years with the court, he won **"The Outstanding Case of the Year Award."**

He currently writes a blog for **Psychology Today**. The name of his blog is, **"Can't We All Just Get Along?"**